TOWARDS A NEW MANIFESTO

TOWARDS A
NEW MANIFESTO

THEODOR ADORNO
& MAX HORKHEIMER

Translated by
Rodney Livingstone

VERSO
London • New York

First published by Verso 2011
Translation © Rodney Livingstone 2011
Originally published under the title 'Diskussion über Theorie und Praxis', an appendix to vol. 13 of Max Horkheimer, *Gesammelte Schriften, Nachgelassene Schriften 1949–1972*
© S. Fischer 1989

1 3 5 7 9 10 8 6 4 2

Verso
UK: 6 Meard Street, London W1F 0EG
US: 20 Jay Street, Suite 1010, Brooklyn, NY 11201
www.versobooks.com

Verso is the imprint of New Left Books

ISBN-13: 978-1-84467-819-8

British Library Cataloguing in Publication Data
A catalogue record for this book is available
from the British Library

Library of Congress Cataloging-in-Publication Data
A catalog record for this book is available
from the Library of Congress

Typeset in Minion by Hewer UK Ltd, Edinburgh
Printed in the US by Maple Vail

CONTENTS

Introduction to
Adorno & Horkheimer

A life-long intellectual partnership between two major thinkers, so close that their most celebrated single texts were co-authored and their names are difficult to dissociate, is rare enough to rank as virtually a sport of history. There seem to be only two cases: in the nineteenth century, Marx and Engels, and in the twentieth century, Horkheimer and Adorno. Might they be regarded as prefigurations of what in a post-bourgeois world would become less uncommon? Their patterns differed. Marx and Engels, born two years apart, were contemporaries; once their friendship was formed, collaboration between them never ceased. Adorno was eight years Horkheimer's junior, and a close working relationship came much later, with many more vicissitudes: initial meeting in 1921, intermittent friction and exchange up to the mid-1930s, concord only in American exile from 1938 onwards, more pointedly distinct identities throughout. The general trajectory of the Frankfurt Institute for Social Research is well known, as over time 'critical theory'—originally Horkheimer's code-word for Marxism—confined itself to the realms of philosophy, sociology and aesthetics; to all appearances completely detached from politics. Privately it was otherwise, as the exchange below makes clear.

This unique document is the record, taken down by Gretel Adorno, of discussions over three weeks in the spring of 1956, with a view to the production of—as Adorno puts it—a contemporary version of The Communist Manifesto. *In form it might be described, were jazz not anathema to Adorno, as a philosophical jam-session, in which the two thinkers improvise freely, often wildly, on central themes of their work—theory and practice, labour and leisure, domination and freedom—in a political register found nowhere else in their writing. Amid a careening flux of arguments, aphorisms and asides, in which the trenchant alternates with the reckless, the playful with the ingenuous, positions are swapped and contradictions unheeded, without any compulsion for consistency. In substance, each thinker reveals a different profile. Horkheimer, historically more politicized, was by now the more conservative, imbibing* Time *on China, if not yet to the point where he would commend the Kaiser for warning of the Yellow Peril. Though still blaming the West for what went wrong with the Russian Revolution, and rejecting any kind of reformism, his general outlook was now close to Kojève's a decade later: 'We can expect nothing more from mankind than a more or less worn-out version of the American system'. Adorno, more aesthetically minded, emerges paradoxically as the more radical: reminding Horkheimer of the need to oppose Adenauer, and envisaging their project as a 'strictly Leninist manifesto', even in a period when 'the horror is that for the first time we live in a world in which we can no longer imagine a better one'.*

Publisher's note

1

The Role of Theory

1. *Never was sociology as bankrupt as it is today with the idea of the doubling of the world.*

2. Sub specie aeternitatis: *all will be well (even if the party no longer exists).*

3. *Work has been called on to replace the belief that all will be well.*

AD 1   [Never was sociology as bankrupt as it is today with the idea of the doubling of the world.]

HORKHEIMER: What we see today is a doubling of the world.

ADORNO: That is exactly Marx's epistemology. He said that the task of theory is to reflect reality. [1]

HORKHEIMER: Indeed, reflect the way it looks from the situation of the proletariat. Developments in this so-called Western hemisphere have led to the growing tendency to translate thought into scientific statement. You end up with nothing more than a few clichés, such as freedom or

---

1   See for example the statement: 'Only after this work [of research] has been done can the real movement be appropriately presented. If this is done successfully, if the life of the subject-matter is now reflected back in the ideas . . .' Karl Marx, *Capital*, vol. 1, trans. Ben Fowkes, Postface to the Second Edition, The Pelican Marx Library, Harmondsworth 1976, p. 102.

religion. A further factor is that we no longer have either the bourgeoisie or the proletariat, which might have taken its place. From a certain point on the bourgeoisie has to double itself. In contrast, the workers still had a utopia. Then Marx came along and took away their utopia with the aid of the doubling process. On the one hand, he brought them closer to reality; but he then did away with the tension with reality.

ADORNO: The motif of subjectivism. [Its] link with positivism.

HORKHEIMER: The form taken by immiseration has undergone great changes.

ADORNO: It must be said that even so subjective consciousness cannot simply be reduced to insignificance. That's what is done by the type of Marxism that becomes rigidly dogmatic and really does turn into the ideology of existing conditions. If a worker no longer notices that he is a worker, this has important implications for theory.

HORKHEIMER: The entire rationale for theory seems to have disappeared because on the one hand the bourgeoisie transforms thought into facts and on the other the party no longer exists.

ADORNO: The Russians too no longer have any theory but only mumbo-jumbo and positivism.

AD 2   [*Sub specie aeternitatis*: all will be well (even if the party no longer exists).]

ADORNO: Reason, which is essential to keep the machinery in motion, necessarily contains its other. When you start to think, you cannot stop short at purely reproductive thinking. This does not mean that things will really work out like that, but you cannot think without thinking that otherness. The general stultification today is the direct result of cutting out utopia. When you reject utopia, thought itself withers away. Thought is killed off in the mere doubling process.

HORKHEIMER: Language is urbanity. The role of towns.[2] Whatever is right about human society is embedded in the language – the idea that all will be well. When you open your mouth to speak, you always say that too. [3]

ADORNO: The idea of truth transcends positivity.

---

2 'Role of towns' is a handwritten insertion.

3 Horkheimer had already put this view to Adorno in a letter of 14 September 1941 (see Horkheimer, *Gesammelte Schriften*, vol. 17, p. 168ff.).

HORKHEIMER: And for something to be true means that it is so constituted that everyone must acknowledge it.

ADORNO: The entire mess today arises from a subjectivity that is ignorant of itself, that mistakes itself for objectivity. The idea of the good that is tacitly assumed in the theory stems from the fact that thought necessarily includes the element of reflection. This cushions the effect of our actions. Just as the imagination developed out of the age-old misdeeds of biology among other things, helping to strip them of their demonic aspect, in the same way theory contains an anti-mythological dimension. This means that because we pause to reflect we do not just lash out blindly. A person who thinks does not just react with his fists, does not just devour things unthinkingly. The time lag caused by the moment of reflection between hunger, fury and lashing out is the origin of the idea that all will be well. By confronting the ends with the means something necessarily comes into being that brings about the suspension of the entire blindness and immediacy. For me to master nature, I have to think. But by thinking, I interpose a medium between the object of action and myself that strives to go beyond both. The gesture of the savage who pauses for an instant to reflect whether or not he wishes to eat his prisoner contains teleologically the end of violence.

HORKHEIMER: My own thoughts are far more modest; I simply say that when I speak, I postulate my subject as the universal. By speaking, I eliminate the particularity of the subject. Dewey says every act of thought contains the following element: what I say here can be said only by someone who does not really possess the whole and cannot know it. I simply put it forward for debate. Whether it is right or not will emerge in the course of the historical process of discussion.[4]

ADORNO: Artists too are actually no more than the instruments that carry something out.

HORKHEIMER: Subjectivism consists in the fact that whatever makes use of the individual subject does not distinguish itself from that subject but merely interprets it subjectively.

AD 3 [Work has been called on to replace the belief that all will be well.]

HORKHEIMER: Labour is what mediates

---

4   See John Dewey, *Essays in Experimental Logic*. Parts of this appear as Chapter XVI, 'Thinking and Meaning', in Dewey, *Intelligence in the Modern World*, ed. Joseph Ratner, New York 1939, p. 842.

between human beings. The 'process of civilization' has been fetishized.[5]

ADORNO: In Marx's chapter on fetishism, the social relation appears in the form of the exchange principle, as if it were the thing in itself.

HORKHEIMER: The instrument becomes the main thing.

ADORNO: But our task is to explain this by speculating on labour's ultimate origins, to infer it from the principle of society, so that it

---

5 What follows are extracts from a transcript of discussions between Adorno and Horkheimer, dated between 12 March and 2 April 1956, which took place in Frankfurt. Reprinted with permission of Fischer Verlag from Max Horkheimer, *Gesammelte Schriften*, vol. 19: *Nachträge, Verzeichnisse und Register*, Frankfurt 1996, pp. 37–71. Section headings and footnotes are by the volume's editor, Gunzelin Schmid Noerr, unless otherwise indicated.

goes beyond Marx. Because exchange value seems to be absolute, the labour that has created it seems to be absolute too, and not the thing for whose sake it basically exists. In actuality the subjective aspect of use value conceals the objective utopia, while the objectivity of exchange value conceals subjectivism.

HORKHEIMER: Work is the key to making sure that 'all will be well'. But by elevating it to godlike status, it is emptied of meaning.

ADORNO: How does it come about that work is regarded as an absolute? Work exists to control the hardships of life, to ensure the reproduction of mankind. The success of labour stands in a problematic relationship to the effort required. It does not necessarily or certainly reproduce the lives of those who work but only of those who induce others to work for them. In order to persuade human beings to work you have to fob them off with the waffle about work as the thing in itself.

HORKHEIMER: That's how it is among the bourgeoisie. This was not the attitude of the Greeks. The young worker on the motorbike treats work as his god because he enjoys riding the bike so much.

ADORNO: But even if he really does enjoy it, that subjective happiness still remains ideology.

HORKHEIMER: But if you were to tell him about our idea that it is supposed to be enjoyable, he would find that hard to understand and would rather we left him in peace.

ADORNO: All that is delusion.

HORKHEIMER: Yes and no. It really does call for great effort.

ADORNO: So does riding a motorbike.

HORKHEIMER: That is an objectively measurable effort; he is happy to make it. His true pleasure in motorbike riding is in the anal sounds it emits. We just look foolish if we try to give explanations that are too precise.

ADORNO: Work figures as early as the Bible.

HORKHEIMER: Initially as the exchange principle.

ADORNO: But it is still unclear why work should be cathected in the first place.

HORKHEIMER: It is also the worst punishment for someone not to be allowed to work at all.

ADORNO: Concentration camps are a key to all these things. In the society we live in all work is like the work in the camps.

HORKHEIMER: Take care, you risk coming close to the idea of enjoying work. The uselessness of the work and derision deprive people of the last bit of pleasure they might obtain from it, but I do not know if that is the crucial factor. No ideology survives in the camps. Whereas our society still insists that work is good.

ADORNO: How does work come to be an end in itself? This dates back to a time far earlier than capitalism. Initially, I suppose, because society reproduced itself through labour, but then in each individual case the relation between concrete labour and reproduction is opaque. In socially useful labour people have to forget what it is good for. The abstract necessity of labour is expressed in the fact that value is ascribed to labour in itself.

HORKHEIMER: I do not believe that human beings naturally enjoy working, no matter whether their work has a purpose or not. Originally, the position of man is like that of a dog you want to train. He would like to return to an earlier state of being. He works in order not to have to work. The reification of labour is a stage in the process that enables us to return to childhood, but at a higher level.

ADORNO: It has a positive and a negative side. The positive side lies in the teleology that work potentially makes work superfluous; the negative side is that we succumb to the mechanism of reification, in the course of which we forget the best thing of all. That turns a part of the process into an absolute. But it is not an aberration, since without it the whole process wouldn't function.

HORKHEIMER: It is not just a matter of ideology, but is also influenced by the fact that a shaft of light from the telos falls onto labour. Basically, people are too short-sighted. They misinterpret the light that falls on labour from ultimate goals. Instead, they take labour qua labour as the telos and hence see their personal work success as that purpose. That is the secret. If they did not do that, such a thing as solidarity would be possible. A shaft of light from the telos falls on the means to achieve it. It is just as if instead of worshipping their lover they worship the house in which she dwells. That, incidentally, is the source of all poetry.

ADORNO: The whole of art is always both true and false. We must not succumb to the ideology of work, but we cannot deny that all happiness is twinned with work.

HORKHEIMER: The shaft of light must be reflected back by an act of resistance.

ADORNO: The animal phase in which one does nothing at all cannot be retrieved.

HORKHEIMER: Happiness would be an animal condition viewed from the perspective of whatever has ceased to be animal.

ADORNO: Animals could teach us what happiness is.

HORKHEIMER: To achieve the condition of an animal at the level of reflection—that is freedom. Freedom means not having to work.

ADORNO: Philosophy always asserts that freedom is when you can choose your own work, when you can claim ownership of everything awful.

HORKHEIMER: That's the product of fear. In the East they have realized that freedom of this sort is not such a big deal, and that's why they have chosen slavery instead. The main point there is that justice should prevail; they set no store by freedom. Freedom would mean reverting to a diffuse state of affairs at a higher level. Since civilization is identical with labour, idolizing the one is as bad as idolizing the other. The chaotic, the diffuse—that would be happiness.

2

Work, Spare Time and Freedom—I

12 March, a.m.

HORKHEIMER: Teddie wants to rescue a pair of concepts: theory and practice. These concepts are themselves obsolete.

ADORNO: Discrepancy between murdering the Jews, burying them alive because they weren't worth the second bullet, and the theory that is expected to change the world.

HORKHEIMER: Two opposing beliefs: the faith in progress, cherished also by

Marxism, and the view that history cannot achieve it.

ADORNO: But that is not the nub of the disagreement between us.

HORKHEIMER: Your view is that we should live our lives in such a way that things will get better in a hundred years. That's more or less what the parson says too.

ADORNO: Our disagreement is about whether history can succeed or not. How are we to interpret the 'can'? On the one hand, the world contains opportunities enough for success. On the other hand, everything is bewitched, as if under a spell. If the spell could be broken, success would be a possibility. If people want to persuade us that the conditional nature of man sets limits to utopia, that is simply untrue. The possibility of a completely unshackled reality remains valid. In a world in which senseless suffering has ceased to exist, Schopenhauer is wrong.

HORKHEIMER: In the long run things cannot change. The possibility of regression is always there. That means we have to reject both Marxism and ontology. Neither the good nor the bad remains, but the bad is more likely to survive. The critical mind must free itself from a Marxism which says that all will be well if only you become a socialist. We can expect nothing more from mankind than a more or less worn-out version of the American system. The difference between us is that Teddie still retains a certain penchant for theology. My own thoughts tend to move in the direction of saying that good people are dying out. In the circumstances, planning would offer the best prospect.

ADORNO: If the result of planning was that beggars would cease to exist, then planning itself would shed its rigidity, and decisive change would be the result.

HORKHEIMER: Perhaps, but a relapse into barbarism is no less conceivable.

ADORNO: Relapse into barbarism is always an option. If the world were so planned that everything one did served the whole of society in a transparent manner, and senseless activities were abandoned, I would be happy to spend two hours a day working as a lift attendant.

HORKHEIMER: An assertion of that kind leads us directly to reformism.

ADORNO: Reform of the administration cannot be brought about by peaceful means.

HORKHEIMER: That is not so important. After the revolution there will be no certainty that it won't relapse once again. Both Marxism and the bourgeois world take good care to make sure that people cannot revert to the pre-civilized phase, the phase in which man has sought refuge from work by reverting to childhood.

ADORNO: Spare-time activities.

HORKHEIMER: Man is worth something only as long as he works. This is where the concept of freedom comes in.

ADORNO: Freedom from work.

HORKHEIMER: Freedom is not the freedom to accumulate, but the fact that I have no need to accumulate.

ADORNO: That's something you can find in
    Marx. On the one hand, Marx imagined liber-
    ation from work. On the other, social labour is
    seen in a very bright light. The two ideas are
    not properly articulated. Marx did not criti-
    cize the ideology of labour, because he needed
    the concept of labour in order to be able to
    settle accounts with the bourgeoisie.

HORKHEIMER: We are in need of a dialectic
    here. People repress their own chaotic drives
    which might lead them away from work. This
    is what makes them feel that work is sacred.

ADORNO: The idea of freedom from labour is
    replaced by the possibility of choosing one's
    own work. Self-determination means that
    within the division of labour already laid
    down I can slip into the sector that promises
    me the greatest rewards.

HORKHEIMER: The idea that freedom consists in self-determination is really rather pathetic, if all it means is that the work my master formerly ordered me to do is the same as the work I now seek to carry out of my own free will; the master did not determine his own actions.

ADORNO: The concept of self-determination has nothing to do with freedom. According to Kant, autonomy means obeying oneself.

HORKHEIMER: A misunderstanding of feudalism.

ADORNO: A necessary false consciousness, ideology.

HORKHEIMER: German idealism, bourgeois ideology: the absolute positing of the semblance of self-determination in feudalism from the standpoint of the bourgeoisie.

ADORNO: Transcendental apperception:[6] labour
made absolute. Labour, which is a prescribed
relationship within society, is reinterpreted to
signify freedom.

HORKHEIMER: Barbaric punishments in the
Soviet zone for people who fail to fulfil their
norms. This is directly connected to the ideology of consumption in both halves of the
world. The opposite of work is regarded as
nothing more than consumption.

ADORNO: Karl Kraus said that man was not
created as a consumer or as a producer but as
a human being.[7]

---

6   In Kant this is the purely formal, original, constantly
identical self-consciousness that is presupposed in all ideas
and concepts. See the *Critique of Pure Reason*, trans. Paul
Guyer and Allen W. Wood, §16, 'On the original synthetic
unity of apperception', Cambridge 1997, p. 246ff.

7   Karl Kraus, *Die Fackel*, nos. 406–412, 5 October 1915, p. 96.

HORKHEIMER: Nowadays people prefer to talk of social partners.

ADORNO: All antitheses are put into the same basket nowadays.

HORKHEIMER: We are in favour of the chaotic, of that which has not been included.

ADORNO: You can't advocate the chaotic. Example of Engels's stuffiness.

HORKHEIMER: We have not yet discovered why it has always been supposed to be so terrible in bourgeois society, as far back as Rome, for a man inflamed by desire to touch a woman's body. It is connected with the best and the worst in them. The revulsion from the world of exchange has found refuge there. The non-bourgeois is supposed to preserve itself in love.

ADORNO: I suppose that bourgeois sexual taboos are connected with the *jus primae noctis*. Women should acquire the right to dispose of their own bodies. Human beings become their own property. That is threatened by sexuality and this sets the scene for the perennial war between the sexes.

HORKHEIMER: Kant's definition of marriage.[8] Love probably contains the false negation of bourgeois society.

ADORNO: It negates it in an impotent fashion, perpetuating it through its negation.

HORKHEIMER: The world is dominated by

8   According to Kant, marriage is 'the union of two persons of different sexes for lifelong possession of each other's sexual attributes': *Metaphysics of Morals*, ed. Mary Gregor, Cambridge 1996, p. 62.

one long hymn to work, but this too is not merely negative. Machiavelli.

ADORNO: Happiness is connected to work.

HORKHEIMER: The worst thing is to mix up work and happiness.

ADORNO: Effort is an integral part of sexual happiness. It is true enough that work is also happiness, but one isn't allowed to say so. Or do we only find happiness in our work because we ourselves are bourgeois?

HORKHEIMER: Freud. Death drive.

3

Work, Spare Time and Freedom—II

12 March, p.m.

HORKHEIMER: Thesis: nowadays we have enough by way of productive forces; it is obvious that we could supply the entire world with goods and could then attempt to abolish work as a necessity for human beings. In this situation it is mankind's dream that we should do away with both work and war. The only drawback is that the Americans will say that if we do so, we shall arm our enemies. And in fact, there is a kind of dominant stratum in the East compared to which John Foster Dulles is an amiable innocent.

ADORNO: We ought to include a section on
the objection: what will people do with all
their free time?

HORKHEIMER: In actual fact their free time
does them no good because the way they have
to do their work does not involve engaging
with objects. This means that they are not
enriched by their encounter with objects.
Because of the lack of true work, the subject
shrivels up and in his spare time he is nothing.

ADORNO: Because people have to work so
hard, there is a sense in which they spend their
spare time obsessively repeating the rituals of
the efforts that have been demanded of them.
We must not be absolutely opposed to work.

HORKHEIMER: We ought to construct a kind
of programme for a new form of practice. In
the East people degenerate into beasts of

burden. Coolies probably had to do less work than today's workers in six or seven hours.

ADORNO: 'No herdsman and one herd.'[9] A kind of false classless society. Society finds itself on the way to what looks like the perfect classless society but is in reality the very opposite.

HORKHEIMER: That's too reactionary. We still have to say something to explain why mankind has to pass through this atomistic stage of civilization. Nowadays people say: treat us nicely and productivity will rise. The fact that this is said openly is worth a good deal in itself.

ADORNO: The reason why this entire question of spare time is so unfortunate is that people

---

9 'No herdsman and one herd. Everyone wants the same thing. Everything is the same; whoever thinks otherwise goes voluntarily into the madhouse.' Friedrich Nietzsche, *Thus Spoke Zarathustra*, Harmondsworth 1961, p. 46.

unconsciously mimic the work process, whereas what they really want is to stop working altogether. Happiness necessarily presupposes the element of effort. Basically, we should talk to mankind once again as in the eighteenth century: you are upholding a system that threatens to destroy you. The appeal to class won't work any more, since today you are really all proletarians. One really has to think about whom one is addressing.

HORKHEIMER: The Western world.

ADORNO: We know nothing of Asia.

HORKHEIMER: What are we to say to the Western world? You must deliver food to the East?

ADORNO: The introduction of fully fledged socialism, third phase in the various countries.

Everything hinges on that. What about the *Communist Manifesto* as a theme for variations?

HORKHEIMER: The world situation is that everything seems to be improving, but the world's liberators all look like Cesare Borgia.

ADORNO: I have the feeling that, under the banner of Marxism, the East might overtake Western civilization. This would mean a shift in the entire dynamics of history. Marxism is being adopted in Asia in much the same way as Christianity was taken up in Mexico at one time. Europe too will probably be swallowed up at some point in the future.

HORKHEIMER: I believe that Europe and America are probably the best civilizations that history has produced up to now as far as prosperity and justice are concerned. The key point now is to ensure the preservation of these gains. That can be achieved only if we remain ruthlessly critical of this civilization.

ADORNO: We cannot call for the defence of the Western world.

HORKHEIMER: We cannot do so because that would destroy it. If we were to defend the Russians, that's like regarding the invading Teutonic hordes as morally superior to the [Roman] slave economy. We have nothing in common with Russian bureaucrats. But they stand for a greater right as opposed to Western culture. It is the fault of the West that the Russian Revolution went the way it did. I am always terribly afraid that if we start talking about politics, it will produce the kind of discussion that used to be customary in the Institute.

ADORNO: Discussion should at all costs avoid a debased form of Marxism. That was connected with a specific kind of positivist tactic, namely the sharp divide between ideas and substance.

HORKHEIMER: That mainly took the form of too great an insistence on retaining the terminology.

ADORNO: But this has to be said. They still talk as if a far-left splinter group were on the point of rejoining the Politburo tomorrow.

HORKHEIMER: What are the implications of that for our terminology? As soon as we start arguing with the Russians about terminology we are lost.

ADORNO: On the other hand, we must not abandon Marxist terminology.

HORKHEIMER: We have nothing else. But I am not sure how far we must retain it. Is the political question still relevant at a time when you cannot act politically?

ADORNO: On the one hand, it is ideology, on the other, all processes that might lead to change are political processes. Politics is both ideology and genuine reality.

HORKHEIMER: You spoke in the subjunctive; you evidently do not really believe in these processes.

ADORNO: My innermost feeling is that at the moment everything has shut down, but it could all change at a moment's notice. My own belief is as follows: this society is not moving towards a welfare state. It is gaining increasing control over its citizens but this control grows in tandem with the growth in its irrationality. And the combination of the two is constitutive. As long as this tension persists, you cannot arrive at the equilibrium that would be needed to put an end to all spontaneity. I cannot imagine a world intensified to the point of insanity without objective oppositional forces being unleashed.

HORKHEIMER: But I can. Because mankind is destroying itself. The world is mad and will remain so. When it comes down to it, I find it easy to believe that the whole of world history is just a fly caught in the flames.

ADORNO: The world is not just mad. It is mad and rational as well.

HORKHEIMER: The only thing that goes against my pessimism is the fact that we still carry on thinking today. All hope lies in thought. But it is easy to believe that it could all come to an end.

ADORNO: And that no one will carry on thinking. But even Mr Eisenhower will be unable to choose Nixon as his running mate for fear of a preventive war.[10]

HORKHEIMER: Perhaps. But what is that compared to the murder of twenty million Chinese?[11]

ADORNO: The fact is that there is an authority that has the potential to prevent total catastrophe. This authority must be appealed to. It is

---

10   Presumably a reference to the 1956 US Presidential election.

11   Horkheimer is probably referring to a blood-curdling *Time* magazine cover story: 'China: High Tide of Terror', 5 March 1956; he kept a copy of this issue in his archive.

the instinct in American voters that would refuse to tolerate Richard Nixon as Vice President.

HORKHEIMER: That is a reformist position.

ADORNO: I have the feeling that what we are doing is not without its effect.

HORKHEIMER: More or less, depending on whether we have a clear idea of what ought to be done. We cannot rely on the assumption that people will still have any memories of socialism. That can easily lead to arrogant criticism of the kind practised by Marx and Karl Kraus, where you have the feeling that their criticism is based on a mistaken theory. That only strengthens the wicked. What is dubious about Kraus is a kind of crowing, because whatever underlies his position is not something we can approve of. We have to defend the view that the West should produce so that no one will go hungry.

ADORNO: This must first be applied to the West itself.

HORKHEIMER: What should happen? In France, for example?[12] Should they make better laws?

ADORNO: Recorder culture is spreading throughout Europe. We shall hear tomorrow that Rosenstock-Huessy has been made adviser to Eisenhower. [13]

---

12   Evidently a reference to the Algerian War that had begun in 1954. The war reached a critical point in 1956 (when there were strikes by Algerian workers in France) when a debate in the National Assembly lasting several days ended with granting extensive powers to the government.

13   Eugen Rosenstock-Huessy (1888–1973), legal historian and sociologist, 1923–33 professor in Breslau. He emigrated to the USA where he taught at various

HORKHEIMER: How would it be if we were to
withdraw to the position of saying that we want
to see to it that as much as possible of this
Western culture is taken over into the next
stage of history, in particular the tradition of
rationality.

---

universities. From 1950 he obtained guest professorships
in a number of Federal German universities; he was also
involved in adult education (such as the founding of the
Academy of Labour in Frankfurt am Main). The Adorno–
Horkheimer correspondence contains the following
assessment of Rosenstock-Huessy by Adorno (at issue
was his suitability for the post of director at an institute
for interdisciplinary studies of art and sociology): 'Eugen
Rosentock-Huessy is undoubtedly a highly intelligent
man . . . He comes, as you probably know, from the
Patmos Circle and at least in his earlier years he was
associated with a certain authoritarian religiosity. I do
not believe that he possesses authentic freedom and in a
higher sense the progressive attitude that is so important
particularly in matters concerning relations between art
and society, where cultural conservatives like to disport
themselves.' (Letter of 2 February 1953, Max Horkheimer
Archive: vol. 6 1E, p. 275).

ADORNO: We cannot advocate that. Schelsky is simultaneously stupid and shrewd.[14]

HORKHEIMER: In addition to work we still have the concept of freedom.

ADORNO: On the one hand, we are facing questions today that can no longer simply be expressed in economic terms; on the other hand, anthropological questions can no longer be separated from economic ones.

HORKHEIMER: Today it is no longer possible to distinguish between good and bad.

---

14   Helmut Schelsky (1912–1984) was a sociologist who taught in Hamburg (1949–60) and subsequently in Münster and Bielefeld.

4

The Idea of Mankind

13 March, a.m.

HORKHEIMER: I do not believe that things will turn out well, but the idea that they might is of decisive importance.

ADORNO: That is connected with rationality. Human beings do things in a far more terrible way than animals, but the idea that things might be otherwise is one that has occurred only to humans.

HORKHEIMER: Individual humans, not mankind.

ADORNO: Isn't that really a matter of chance? What is crucial is that the species is so constituted that it carries forward the idea of permanence, and this drives it on to the further idea that violence is not necessary. Once you start to reflect on the motif of self-preservation, you must necessarily go beyond it, because you will soon realize that uninhibited self-preservation always ends up in destruction.

HORKHEIMER: I find it repellent for people to believe that if only everyone could agree, something essential would have been achieved. In reality, the whole of nature should tremble at the thought. The truth is, on the contrary, that all will be well only as long as they keep one another in check.

ADORNO: That would be true of the fraternization among the leaders, a world monopoly. It would be better if the peoples could achieve it.

HORKHEIMER: That would be just as bad. Every new generation has to become civilized all over again.

ADORNO: I don't believe that entirely. I believe that there is a kind of progressive process of higher differentiation. People only become Khrushchevs because they keep getting hit over the head.

HORKHEIMER: That is exactly Herbert Marcuse's position.

ADORNO: I do not believe that human beings are evil when they come into the world.

HORKHEIMER: They are neither good nor evil. They just want to survive.

ADORNO: They are not as bad as all that by nature.

HORKHEIMER: The way it has always been formulated hitherto is a superstition. Superstition is always the belief in evil. It is not the case that human beings will end up understanding one another and everything will be idyllic. But we have to rescue the idea you have put forward there.

ADORNO: Isn't what human beings do to nature a projection of what they do to one another? Hitting out at the outside world because they are always being humiliated?

HORKHEIMER: It's possible. The impotence of this idea is connected with the fact that up to now it has always been poorly formulated. It is perhaps necessary to give conscious expression to an error in which one believes. As Kant said: one really has to believe, in opposition to one's own reason.[15]

ADORNO: In his writings the attempts at mediation are very artificial.

HORKHEIMER: Our question is, in whose interest do we write, now that there is no longer a party and the revolution has become such an unlikely prospect? My answer would be that we should measure everything against the idea that all should be well. We shall probably be unable to do anything else. It is all tied up with language. Everything intellectual is connected

---

15   In the Preface to the second edition of the *Critique of Pure Reason*, Kant states: 'Thus I had to deny knowledge in order to make room for faith . . .' *Critique of Pure Reason*, p. 117.

to language. It is in language that the idea
that all should be well can be articulated.

ADORNO: In Marx language plays no role, he
is a positivist. Kant is not only ideology. His
work contains at some level an appeal to the
species, to mankind as opposed to the limita-
tions of the particular. In his philosophy the
idea of freedom is defined as the idea of
mankind. There is also the implied statement
that the question about whether humans are
merely natural beings is essentially tied to the
relation to nature that characterizes the
isolated individual. He had already noticed
that the concept of freedom does not lie in the
isolated subject, but can be grasped only in
relation to the constitution of mankind as a
whole. Freedom truly consists only in the
realization of humanity as such.

5

The False Abolition of Work

15 March, a.m.

HORKHEIMER: The bourgeois do not succeed entirely in being feudal; they create their own nobility through their labour. I believe that people can pass beyond something only when they are completely captivated by it ideologically. This explains the hymns to labour and the fact that people are so passionate about riding motorbikes. People are nothing more than workers.

ADORNO: They feel that their own congealed labour power is at their disposal. Pleasure in bike riding: DIY, moving around quickly.

HORKHEIMER: Speed is an aspect of work, speeding things up.

ADORNO: The enjoyment of speed is a proxy for the enjoyment of work.

HORKHEIMER: Prison labour. When work is used as a punishment it is hard to prevent it from becoming a pleasure despite everything. You have to make it as unpleasant as possible.

ADORNO: The more superfluous a job of work is, the worse it becomes, the more it degenerates into ideology.

HORKHEIMER: And the more it is misapplied. Work today is not superfluous as long as people still go hungry. Work is perverted. Automation. We should take greater care to help others, to export the right goods to the right people, to seek cures for the sick. Nowadays there is a false abolition of work.

ADORNO: It amounts to production for its own sake.

HORKHEIMER: I couldn't care less about sending spacecraft to the moon.

ADORNO: There is nothing sacred about technology.

HORKHEIMER: Marx already has the idea that in a false society, technology develops wrongly.

ADORNO: There are countless fields where technology could be properly applied. The goods made available nowadays are a kind of pseudo-consumer goods; exchange value is substituted for use value.

HORKHEIMER: People like advertisements. They do what the ads tell them and they know that they are doing so. American magazines and comics.

ADORNO: If I had said to my father that mass culture is untrue, he would have answered: but I enjoy it. Renunciation of utopia means somehow or other deciding in favour of a thing even though I know perfectly well that it is a swindle. That is the root of the trouble.

HORKHEIMER: Because the strength you need to do the right thing is kept on a leash. If we formulate the issues just as we speak, it all sounds too argumentative. People might say that our views are just all talk, our own perceptions. To whom shall we say these things?

ADORNO: We are not proposing any particular course of action. What we want is for people who read what we write to feel the scales falling from their eyes.

HORKHEIMER: People will say, well, this is just philosophers talking. Or else, you have to be like Heidegger and speak like an oracle. We have to solve the problem of theory and practice through our style. We have to make sure that people don't just say, 'My God, the things they say make everything sound very bad, but they don't really mean it like that, even when they shout and curse.' This is all connected with the fact that a party no longer exists.

ADORNO: I see no way out, apart from making these considerations explicit. There is a particular way of writing that offends against specific taboos. You have to find the point that wounds. Offending against sexual taboos.

HORKHEIMER: Marcuse, take care.

ADORNO: The focus on genitality has an element of hostility to pleasure.

HORKHEIMER: I take the opposite view. The more eager one is to break the taboo, the more harmless it is. The more specific your aim, the more powerful the effect. Join the CDU, but make that possible also for deserters. One must be very down to earth, measured and considered so that the impression that something or other is not possible does not arise. We have to actualize the loss of the party by saying, in effect, that we are just as bad as before but that we are playing on the instrument the way it has to be played today.

ADORNO: There is something seductive about that idea—but what is the instrument?

HORKHEIMER: If we could only say that we are fighting a rearguard action. We could perhaps indicate that people are not yet fully aware that they are heading for a situation compared to which Nazism was a relatively modest affair. If we were to tell the Social Democrats today that they should become Communists, that would be quite harmless. But if we were to tell them that they had betrayed bourgeois ideals, that would cease to be so harmless, because the Social Democrats represent the good conscience of our world. We don't want people to say that our writings are so terribly radical. Whoever does not work should not be allowed to eat—that's the point at which we must attack the Social Democrats. We must not say 'you did not want the dictatorship of the proletariat', but 'you have betrayed mankind'. Simply to utter the words 'dictatorship of the proletariat' is to form an alliance with Carlo Schmid and Mao Zedong.[16]

ADORNO: *Nomina sunt odiosa*, names hurt.

HORKHEIMER: The radicality of the formulation deprives the statement of its radicality.

---

16   Carlo Schmid (1896–1979): leading member of the Social Democratic Party.

6

Political Concreteness

15 March, p.m.

HORKHEIMER: A Bonaparte will emerge in
Russia who will conquer the whole of Europe,
and in 500 years everything will be just fine.
That's Marcuse's way of thinking.

ADORNO: Perhaps in a time to come another
party will come into being in one country or
another.

HORKHEIMER: We cannot leave open the
question of what we believe in. The section on

work should contain an excursus on the Utopians. For Marx the only yardstick was the restriction of labour time. We have a much more paradoxical view of that.

ADORNO: The Utopians were actually not very utopian at all. But we must not provide a picture of a positive utopia.

HORKHEIMER: Especially when one is so close to despair.

ADORNO: I wouldn't say that. I believe that because everything is so obvious a new political authority will emerge.

HORKHEIMER: Listeners must be able to hear from the tone that all we can do is simply to say this without adding anything.

ADORNO: The belief that it will come is
perhaps a shade too mechanistic. It *can* come;
whether it will come or whether it will go to
the dogs is terribly hard to predict.

HORKHEIMER: Everything we are discussing
is far too abstract for my liking. What view,
for example, are we to take of America?

ADORNO: We have to add that we believe that
things can come right in the end.

HORKHEIMER: People want us to be far
more outspoken. Our critique must make it
clear that nothing will happen unless some
people or other make it happen. Our style
must reveal what we think should happen.
We ought to write in the style of a possible
opposition within the Communist Party.
Should we be for or against America? For or
against the emergence of a European union?

To ridicule American consumerism is disgraceful unless the reader can somehow pick up how such matters should be regarded. Otherwise, it is merely abuse. My instinct is to say nothing if there is nothing I can do. In your view, our task is at the very least to bring out the utopia in the negative picture. I should like to drive things forward to the point where there is greater clarity in the relationship between that utopia and the present reality.

ADORNO: If I prefer to write about music that is because I have all the mediating categories at my disposal. The same could be said of philosophy. But we do not possess such categories in dealing with the internal developments of the political parties in the different countries. One ought to apply them in the areas where one's own experience has the greatest relevance. How would it be if we were to formulate some guiding political principles today?

HORKHEIMER: If we are to present ourselves with such ambitions, we have to be clear about the yardsticks we are applying, otherwise Marx will keep reappearing at the seams. We want the preservation for the future of everything that has been achieved in America today, such as the reliability of the legal system, the drugstores, etcetera. This must be made quite clear whenever we speak about such matters.

ADORNO: That includes getting rid of TV programmes when they are rubbish.

HORKHEIMER: In the first place, it is fantastically difficult to find out what these TV programmes mean for the workers today. In Germany it is probably the most progressive workers who buy TV sets. Secondly, it is already pretty obvious that in German eyes relations with America are already suspect, not those with Russia. We will have to include a sentence or two to the effect that even if American TV programmes are very similar to Russian ones, they do not directly advocate murder. We have to distinguish clearly between our attitudes towards the different countries.

ADORNO: We must somehow manage to suggest such things rather than say them directly.

HORKHEIMER: The Russians are already half-way towards fascism.

ADORNO: If German hearts warm more towards the Russians, that is not just a nega-tive fact. They think the Russians stand for socialism. People are as yet unaware that the Russians are fascists, especially ordinary people. The industrialists and bankers are well aware of it. As for the Americans, people believe that money is the only thing that matters to them.

ADORNO: In the case of Christianity something happened quite early on. Christ himself said, 'Consider the lilies of the field . . .'[17] and St Paul, 'If any will not work . . .'[18] What I don't like about the Gospels is that one is supposed to be stupid.

---

17   'Consider the lilies of the field, how they grow; they toil not, neither do they spin.' Matthew 6, 28.

18   'If any will not work, neither let him eat.' 2 Thessalonians 3, 10.

7

Critique of Argument

24 March

HORKHEIMER: There is a theme I would like to tackle some day: the question of the nature of argument. One can always say anything about anything. It is also linked to the question of theory and practice.

ADORNO: Thinking that renounces argument—Heidegger—switches into pure irrationalism.

HORKHEIMER: One can argue only if there is a practical implication behind it.

ADORNO: If there is a definite pull behind it. Kant.

HORKHEIMER: You can discuss the *Critique of Pure Reason* until there is nothing left.

ADORNO: Its substantiality lies in its arguments. The arguments are what is ephemeral, they then fall away. One can certainly define intelligence. The concept contains a mixture of quite different things. The ability to think in isolation from the subject matter in question, and on the other hand, the insight that comes from a grasp of that subject matter. These two aspects are connected, but the usual concept of intelligence refers simply to the first, while the second, which is what counts, is dragged along under the label of intuition or the like. It must be said that formal intelligence is the necessary but not sufficient attribute, and that intuition is only a type of experience that is

suddenly activated, and is by no means irra-
tional. There ought to be a phenomenology of
intelligence in which it would appear as the
third component, also appearing in the other
two, but in a distorted form.

HORKHEIMER: You mean that when we speak
there is always some kind of goal lying behind
it, the sum of our experiences and sufferings.
There is something indescribably naive about
wanting to treat intelligence in isolation.

ADORNO: But there really is something like
dianoetic virtue—devoting oneself to something for its own sake and doing it justice.[19]

HORKHEIMER: Practice is implicit in justice.

---

19 Aristotle distinguished between ethical and dianoetic
virtues, i.e. practical as opposed to speculative reason.

ADORNO: This brings us to the point where it can be seen that there is something deluded about the separation of theory and practice. Separating these two elements is actually ideology.

HORKHEIMER: What is meant by doing something justice? We need to find a formulation in order to express what that something truly wants. The midwife aspect.

ADORNO: That is also implicit in Hegel's idea of the self-movement of the concept.

HORKHEIMER: The thing has no need of the good. Whereas we, if we wish to help the thing, really do have some good object in mind and regard the thing as in need of help.

ADORNO: The thing stands in need of the

concept. The concept ought really to be the good aspect of the thing.

HORKHEIMER: That is too abstract for me. It's like someone feeling his way in the dark, not knowing that there is a light.

ADORNO: Philosophy exists in order to redeem what you see in the look of an animal. If you feel that an idea is supposed to serve a practical purpose, it slithers into the dialectic. If, on the other hand, your thought succeeds in doing the thing justice, then you cannot really also assert the opposite. The mark of authenticity of a thought is that it negates the immediate presence of one's own interests. True thought is thought that has no wish to insist on being in the right.

HORKHEIMER: When you speak, you always speak for yourself. When you defend a cause, you also defend yourself. To plead on behalf of a specific cause is not necessarily a bad thing. You feel deeply that your own interests are at stake. Everyone feels the injustice that would occur if one were to be extinguished. To plead on behalf of another is also to plead on one's own behalf.

ADORNO: For example, Löwenthal and Hacker.

HORKHEIMER: In the case of students you often miss the feeling that they are speaking on their own behalf.

ADORNO: The mistrust of argument is at bottom what has inspired the Husserls and Heideggers. The diabolical aspect of it is that the abolition of argument means that their writing ends up in tautology and nonsense. Argument has the form of 'Yes, but . . .'

HORKHEIMER: But the 'Yes, but . . .' remains in the service of making something visible in the object itself.

ADORNO: There is something bad about advocacy—arguing means applying the rules of thinking to the matters under discussion. You really mean to say that if you find yourself in the situation of having to explain why something is bad, you are already lost. Alternatively, you end up saying like Mephistopheles: 'Scorn reason, despise learning.' Then you will discover the primordial forces of being.

HORKHEIMER: The USA is the country of argument.

ADORNO: Argument is consistently bourgeois.

HORKHEIMER: It is our cursed duty to marry thinking with right practice.

8

The Concept of Practice

25 March, a.m.

ADORNO: The central issue is how to relate theory and practice in general. You said that the right theory wants what is right. We can go further than that. Firstly, we must say that thinking is a form of practice; when I think, I am doing something. Even the most rarefied form of mental activity contains an element of the practical.

HORKHEIMER: I do not entirely agree with that.

ADORNO: Thinking is a form of behaviour that in a curious way has taken on the appearance of something in which human activity is not involved.

HORKHEIMER: I am reminded of something related to this. You cannot say that adding up is an activity in the same sense as listening to a piece of music. Just as there is a difference between pushing a chair somewhere and sitting on it. The element of rest, of contemplation belongs on the side of theory.

ADORNO: On the other hand, theory's claim to be pure being, purified of action, has something of a delusion about it.

HORKHEIMER: Theory is theory in the authentic sense only where it serves practice. Theory that wishes to be sufficient unto itself is bad theory. On the other hand, it is also bad theory if it exists only in order to produce something or other.

ADORNO: I always come back to the feeling I have when people ask me how I would act as the director of a radio station or as minister of education. I always have to admit to myself that I would be in the greatest possible state of perplexity. The feeling that we know a huge amount, but that for category reasons it is not possible for us to put our knowledge to genuine practical use, is one that has to enter our deliberations.

HORKHEIMER: That does not go far enough. As long as you are working in a society alongside others you cannot fall back on the concept of practice that was still available to Marx. Our situation is that we have to get to grips with the problem of reformism. What is the meaning of practice if there is no longer a party? In that case doesn't practice mean either reformism or quietism?

ADORNO: Our concept of practice is different from Lazarsfeld's.[20] People have always tried to foist onto us a concept that is appropriate for a state of emergency.

HORKHEIMER: Since the Communist Party already exists within society, this means renouncing what we mean by practice. By practice we really mean that we're serious about the idea that the world needs fundamental change. This has to show itself in both thought and action. The practical aspect lies in the notion of difference; the world has to

20   Paul Lazarsfeld (1901–1976): Austrian émigré sociologist, under whom Adorno worked on the Princeton Radio Research project; known for his empirical focus and entrepreneurial bent; Adorno described him as a 'research technician'.

become different. It is not as if we should do something other than thinking, but rather that we should think differently and act differently. Perhaps this practice really just expects us to kill ourselves? We probably have to start from the position of saying to ourselves that even if the party no longer exists, the fact that we are here still has a certain value.

ADORNO: Moreover, we are by no means as unhappy as other people.

HORKHEIMER: And temperamentally we are a long way from wishing to commit suicide.

ADORNO: Precisely because of its exceptional status, theory is a kind of stand-in for happiness. The happiness that would be brought about by practice finds no correlative in today's world apart from the behaviour of the man who sits in a chair and thinks.

HORKHEIMER: That is an Aristotelian view.

ADORNO: It is not true in so far as happiness is only thought and not real, but it is true in the sense that this exceptional status outside the realm of daily routine is a kind of substitute for happiness. And in that sense the difference between thinking and eating roast goose is not so very great. The one thing can stand in for the other.

HORKHEIMER: But eating roast goose is not the same thing as doing theory. Freedom is being allowed to do as you wish. The fact that thinking gives us pleasure is not what justifies the privileging of theory over practice. Where there is no link to practice, thinking is no different from anything else one happens to enjoy. The difference between thinking we approve of and disapprove of is that the thinking we approve of must have a connection to a world set to rights and must look at the world from this perspective. It must relate to the question of how the world is to be made different. If we wish to write about theory and practice we must give a more incisive account of this aspect. Sometimes by practice we mean the fact that everything we think and do should be classified under the heading of change. At other times, we mean by practice whatever relates to the difference between thinking and doing. We must make every effort to ensure that all our thoughts and actions fit in with the first mentioned concept of practice. You, on the other hand, resist the idea that thought might be denied various possibilities by always asking how we are to make a start.

9

No Utopianism

25 March, p.m.

HORKHEIMER: It must not look as if we were
providing a metaphysical gilding for bourgeois desires.[21] It might be objected that what
we call 'change', 'otherness' [*das Andere*], is
nothing but an ideological projection. Whatever appeared desirable on the basis of certain

---

21 An echo of a metaphor used by Werner Sombart, also
deployed on an earlier occasion by Horkheimer. See 'Die
gegenwärtige Lage der Socialphilosophie und die Aufgaben
eines Instituts für Sozialforschung' (1931), in Horkheimer,
Gesammelte Schriften, vol. 3, Frankfurt 1988, p. 26.

social interests is then endowed with the status of 'change' and contrasted with the entire course of world history.

ADORNO: It could be said that Marx and Hegel taught that there are no ideals in the abstract, but that the ideal always lies in the next step, that the entire thing cannot be grasped directly but only indirectly by means of the next step. In other words, what we are doing is pre-dialectical, a leaping out of the dialectic. I would reply that this objection is itself abstract. It applies to a world that has not yet become a totality. Today, however, where everything is included and the world constitutes a unity as far as one can see, the idea of 'otherness' is one whose time has come. We might almost say that the dialectic, which always contains an element of freedom, has come to a full stop today because nothing remains outside it. What

Hegel and Marx called utopianism has been rendered obsolete by the present stage of history. That is because the stage reached by the forces of production really would permit us to eliminate need and because the entire world has been welded together in a single context of delusion and disaster, so that salvation lies only in impulses that lead us out of that totality.

HORKHEIMER: That is a reversion to utopianism.

ADORNO: The critique of utopianism is based on the idea that technology has not advanced sufficiently. No one can maintain that today. Today we have the pure contradiction between the forces and relations of production.

HORKHEIMER: Marx had already made that claim.

ADORNO: But at the time that was probably not yet the case.

HORKHEIMER: But why should we return to bourgeois ideals?

ADORNO: We can show that the things we dislike are for their part the reflexive forms of the form of production.

HORKHEIMER: Marx was opposed only to things he thought obsolete. We in contrast are Romantics.

ADORNO: Marx would have classed television and the motorbike as ideology.

HORKHEIMER: My objection is that everything we adduce to define 'the other' has something ideological about it. Are these not all animal qualities: a not-too-strenuous life, having enough to eat, not having to work from morning to night? Preventing violence being done to man's nature? What is Marx's view of theory and practice?

ADORNO: Whatever is ripe for the time points to the entire prehistory. The concept of prehistory also contains an element of an abstract utopia.

HORKHEIMER: Marx says that classes must be abolished because the time is ripe for it, the forces of production are strong enough.

ADORNO: If we let history go its own way and we just give it a little push, it will end up in a catastrophe for mankind.

HORKHEIMER: Nothing can be done to prevent that except to bring in socialism.

ADORNO: That's what we say too.

HORKHEIMER: If one always refers back to
the idea of measuring everything according to
the image of how one would like things to be,
one arrives at the concept of utopia, of a
theory that does not lead to action. What use
is a theory that does not tell us how to behave
towards the Russians or the United States?
Reality should be measured against criteria
whose capacity for fulfilment can be demon-
strated in a number of already existing,
concrete developments in historical reality.

ADORNO: Is that not just a repetition writ large
of Mr Ehmann's call from the bunker as refugee
father? One ought simply to do what is right.

HORKHEIMER: What these people want from
us is partly pernicious, partly well-intentioned.
It is the belief that the intellectual must be

someone who can really help. It is not enough to say 'I am just thinking . . .'

ADORNO: On the one hand, theory exists to tell us what can be done about establishing communism within a specific power constellation. On the other hand, it is precisely the pressure to think in terms of such alternatives that reduces thinking to such nonsense today. That is an antinomy.

HORKHEIMER: You cannot simply negate this antinomy abstractly. You cannot say that this pressure destroys thought and end up cursing both the pressure and the thought. You then have to say: hands off politics, just keep on being a university professor. Otherwise we shall end up as stoics. Thinking becomes the only pleasure.

ADORNO: The pleasure of thinking is not to be recommended.

HORKHEIMER: Perhaps we should refuse all compromises and say that writing articles as Marx did is pointless today. No doubt, we still believe there can be moments in history when everything might be turned upside down once again. But today we have to declare ourselves defeatists. Not in a fatalistic way, but simply because of the situation we find ourselves in. There is nothing we can do. We should not turn this into a theory, but have to declare that basically we cannot bring about change. We must not act as if we still could.

ADORNO: On the one hand, you said that you believe that a time may come when it will be possible. On the other hand, there is something idiotic about saying this. The idea that it will work out some day is incompatible with Marxism.

HORKHEIMER: If someone says that all will be well one day, this quite fails to reassure me. After all, the twenty million murdered Chinese are dead and that is something that separates us from Marxism. The belief that all will be well cannot reconcile us to the bad things that have happened. It follows that Marxism is basically not possible unless there is the prospect of an immediate revolution. If that is true, then utopia ceases to be a social utopia and in that event our incompatibility with Marxism is enormously increased.

ADORNO: In that case, utopia is metaphysics.

HORKHEIMER: Not metaphysics, but much more immediate. The idea of practice must shine through in everything we write; a curious waiting process, but one that does not have the ability to justify everything that has happened. We have to think of our own form of existence as the measure of what we think.

ADORNO: Shouldn't we really have to think everything out from the beginning? Write a manifesto that will do justice to the current situation. In Marx's day it could not yet be seen that the immanence of society had become total. That means, on the one hand, that one might almost need to do no more than strip off the outer shell; on the other hand, that no one really wants things to be otherwise.

HORKHEIMER: We still have something of a breathing space. We must not lose sight of that in our discussion of theory. We cannot be active politically and yet every word we write is political. We have to say clearly that the Communist Party is not a whit superior to the liberal politicians in the Federal Republic.

The claim that new constellations are possible has echoes of Trotsky.

ADORNO: The fact that art exists is not rendered immaterial by the statement that what really counts is revolution.

HORKHEIMER: Art is actually not different from what we have in mind, but we have to articulate it.

ADORNO: We should not blind ourselves to this.

HORKHEIMER: We need to make explicit matters that Picasso can remain silent about. It must become quite clear from our general position why one can be a communist and yet despise the Russians.

ADORNO: We must be against Adenauer.

HORKHEIMER: But that is only true as long as we list the reasons that make it possible to keep on living in the West. An appeal for the re-establishment of a socialist party.

ADORNO: With a strictly Leninist manifesto.

HORKHEIMER: Then we would be told that such a manifesto could not appear in Russia, while in the United States and Germany it would be worthless. At best, it might have some success in France and Italy. We are not calling on anyone to take action.

ADORNO: Practice is a rationally led activity; that leads ultimately back to theory. Practice is driven on to theory by its own laws.

HORKHEIMER: Theory is, as it were, one of humanity's tools.

ADORNO: That means that theory and practice cannot be separated.

HORKHEIMER: That is conformism.

ADORNO: For a form of behaviour to be practical I must reflect on something or other. If I have the concept of reflection, the concept of practice implicitly postulates that of theory. The two elements are truly separated from each other and inseparable at the same time.

HORKHEIMER: Theory is required to reflect; it must know why.

ADORNO: What makes theory more than a mere instrument of practice is the fact that it reflects on itself, and in so doing it rescinds itself as mere theory.

HORKHEIMER: It can achieve that only by targeting true practice.

ADORNO: Contemplation had a point while it was still directed at an object in a theological sense. You always criticize theory on the grounds that a communist theory is really an absurdity, the pure observation of something that no longer exists. The concept of theory has undermined itself through the overall concept of enlightenment. There is something archaic about the concept of theory.

HORKHEIMER: Marx would say that what we perceive are not ideas but products of human practice, in a twofold sense. Firstly, in the sense that our attention is still taken up by our needs, and secondly, because we regard as nominalistically insoluble something that we are as yet unable to produce with the methods of science.

ADORNO: The fact that human beings have broken out of nature is very remarkable. Not until today, under conditions of monopoly, has the world of animals been reinstated for the benefit of human beings, everything is closed off. The biological leap of the human species is being revoked once more.

10

The Antinomy of the Political

30 March

HORKHEIMER: We have asked about the relationship between theory and practice if there is no longer a party. Now there is no party and this means that two sources of uncertainty are involved, if we continue to operate in the realm of theory. Firstly, because what is produced in the way of theory no longer has anything in common with Marx, with the most advanced class consciousness; our thoughts are no longer a function of the proletariat. Secondly, it seems then as if we are working on a theory for keeping in stock.

ADORNO: In the best case, it is theory as a message in a bottle.

HORKHEIMER: In stock. Perhaps the time will come again when theory can be of use. A theory that has ceased to have any connection with practice is art. What we need to respond to is the question of whether we are doing philosophy as pure construct.

ADORNO: If I had the choice between a construct and the stockroom, I would always choose the construct. To think thoughts because it is fun seems more dignified.

HORKHEIMER: First thesis: the choice between ideas as constructs and ideas in stock.

ADORNO: We have to express this as bluntly as possible without leaving anything obscure.

HORKHEIMER: Even if our theory doesn't directly feed into practice, and even if the link with practice is utterly opaque, it will nevertheless benefit practice somehow or other. Thinking has lost direction in a very crucial way. Philosophy differs from art in this respect. If we speak of the injustice and mendacity of the world in a philosophical text and the world replies that it is not unjust and mendacious, since there is no alternative at present, it is just doing the best it can, this means that there is something wrong with theory. We rightly expect theory to have a definite meaning. In contrast, we just listen to music. Theory cannot be oblivious of itself. Theory as resistance. Basically your thinking too has a highly practical orientation.

ADORNO: I know that everything is false as long as the world is as it is.

HORKHEIMER: You would say that merely to say this is to achieve much. I say that a lot more has to happen. We have to point to the direction we must travel in to make sure that the horrors are no longer necessary. In your view theory has done its job once we can say that. I believe we must retain the aspect of Marxism which insists that it is not enough to say something is bad. In actuality we still have to do battle with the standpoint of the French counter-revolution, which maintains that the work done by the executioner is still needed since otherwise things would be even worse.

ADORNO: What irritates me so much about the entire relationship between theory and practice is something quite obvious, namely the experience that everything the Russians write slips into ideology, into crude, stupid twaddle, that culture is rubbish and that somewhere, at the very same spot as in Marx and Engels, there is an element of re-barbarization. Thinking in their [the Russians'] writings is more reified than in the most advanced bourgeois thought. I have always wanted to rectify that and develop a theory that remains faithful to Marx, Engels and Lenin, while keeping up with culture at its most advanced.

HORKHEIMER: Who would not subscribe to that? You wish to retain culture, but being ruthless and barbaric is necessarily part of this culture. Your attitude has something of Don Quixote about it. You would like to omit whatever doesn't suit you, as if this culture could survive in present conditions without the injustice we both hate.

ADORNO: The ruthless critique of this culture is one element of our own activity.

HORKHEIMER: I do not myself think that pure cultural criticism is so important. An American might well say to us, what do you really want, we are the better human beings, we want to organize things so as to put an end to barbarism. This is what we have to sort out. Do you know what it is about practice that you reject? The recipe. Theory should not be a recipe, but if it remains quite unconnected with any such thing . . .

ADORNO: It negates itself. When ideas become too concrete, I protest; when they become too abstract, you protest. When Marx and Engels wrote the *Communist Manifesto* there was no party either. It is not always necessary to join up with something already in existence.

HORKHEIMER: If you produce revolutionary writings in a non-revolutionary situation without engaging with the positive aspects of a culture, it always seems somehow hopeless.

ADORNO: But Marx did not have the aura of someone who was godforsaken.

HORKHEIMER: There was nothing sectarian about him. We must not write a single word that might fail to acknowledge that we live in this particular society and are a part of it.

ADORNO: We live on the culture we criticize.

HORKHEIMER: I meant the society.

ADORNO: You said that the barbarism of this culture can be countered only with barbaric methods. So are the means neutral towards the ends? In other words, can I really be opposed to barbarism if I myself write like writers in the Marxist tradition?

HORKHEIMER: Karl Kraus is likewise barbaric.

ADORNO: We have to express ourselves in such a way that our readers can see quite clearly how things have to be changed, but one must allow the reader to see enough to enable him to glimpse the idea that change is possible.

HORKHEIMER: Second thesis: What we say today is something implicit in morality or Christianity. If there is so much affluence as there is in the Western world, we must give to those who have nothing.

ADORNO: The fault lies exclusively with ideology. Basically, we have to change consciousness, to dissolve the context of delusion in the minds of others. Then all would be well.

HORKHEIMER: It is not just the state of consciousness. If those who have plenty were to hand some over to the needy, they would ultimately find themselves overwhelmed by them. Human beings live on horror. It's connected with eating meat. Your 'beggar hurries to the gate'[22]—that is the culture we live in.

ADORNO: Theory is already practice. And practice presupposes theory. Today, everything is supposed to be practice and at the same time, there is no concept of practice. We do not live in a revolutionary situation, and actually things are worse than ever. The horror

---

22 From a song in Adorno's *Der Schatz des Indianer-Joe*, Frankfurt 1979, pp. 33–4.

is that for the first time we live in a world in which we can no longer imagine a better one.

HORKHEIMER: The party no longer exists.

ADORNO: Any appeal to form a left-wing socialist party is not on the agenda. Such a party would either be dragged along in the wake of the Communist Party, or it would suffer the fate of the SPD or Labour Party. It is not a political issue that there is no party.

HORKHEIMER: The moment politics is less able to do the right thing than at any time in history is also the moment politics is no longer of relevance.

ADORNO: The problem of he who speaks.

HORKHEIMER: Can it be said that today the political situation is worse than at any other time? It is not just worse. What links the two of us and separates us from other people is a kind of reluctance to say that twenty million are being murdered in China but soon there will be no more famines. What we reject is not practice but telling others what to do. Because we are still permitted to live, we are under an obligation to do something.

11

Individualism

31 March

HORKHEIMER: We believe that human beings
should be subtly different. In Marx socialism
was concerned to ensure that all men would
be equal.

ADORNO: Marx was too harmless; he probably
assumed naively that human beings are essentially identical and that they remain so. And
that once the evil second nature was removed,
all would be well. He did not concern himself
with subjectivity, it didn't really interest him.

He would have dismissed as a milieu theory the idea that people are products of society down to the innermost fibre of their being. Lenin was the first to articulate such a theory.

12

The Historical Change in the Relationship Between Statics and Dynamics

2 April

ADORNO: The antithesis of static and dynamic does not reach the heart of the distinction. The bourgeoisie has long since become dynamic.[23]

---

23 On this all too cryptic remark by Adorno, see also 'Über Statik und Dynamik als soziologische Kategorien' [On static and dynamic as sociological categories'] (1961), in Adorno, *Gesammelte Schriften*, vol. 8, p. 217ff.

TRANSLATED BY RODNEY LIVINGSTONE